I S

THE

WINDOW

OF

NOTHINGNESS

PRAISE FOR RADULESCU'S
ROMANIAN COLLECTIONS

Stella Vinitchi Radulescu's poetry irradiates, like a magnetic field charged with mysteries, the movements and the rituals of her bright vision. One of the strongest characteristics of her poems consists in the unabridged relationship she establishes with words, a pact that sends us to their origins. The poet dares to carry the shadow of her own loneliness, keeping pace with that of her words, up to the line of a horizon where sky and earth, life and death merge.
  —ALEXANDRU LUNGU, editor of *Zarathustra* and *Argo*

Groundbreaking, [Stella Vinitchi Radulescu's poems] give a new spark to freshness, more vigor to femininity, and a seed of doubt to melancholy.
  —ION CARAION, author of *Poems* and *The Error of Being*

I SCRAPE THE WINDOW OF NOTHINGNESS

NEW & SELECTED POEMS

STELLA VINITCHI RADULESCU

ORISON
BOOKS
OrisonBooks.com

ORISON
BOOKS

Orison Books, Inc.
I Scrape the Window of Nothingness: New & Selected Poems
Copyright © 2015 by Stella Vinitchi Radulescu
All rights reserved

ISBN-13: 978-0-9906917-0-9 (hardcover)
ISBN-13: 978-0-9906917-1-6 (paper)
ISBN-13: 978-0-9906917-2-3 (e-book)

For ordering information, please contact:
Ingram Book Group, One Ingram Blvd., La Vergne, TN 37086
(800) 937-8000
orders@ingrambook.com

For permission to reprint poems from this book, contact
Orison Books, PO Box 8385, Asheville, NC 28814
or use the contact form at www.orisonbooks.com/contact.

Grateful acknowledgment is made to the editors of the following periodicals and publications, in which the listed poems from the New Poems section of this collection originally appeared, sometimes in earlier forms: *The Freeman*: "lessons in diving and thirst"; *Ginosko Literary Journal*: "the human condition," "ennui," "heart heart heart," "teaching death to fourth graders"; *Gris-Gris Journal of Literature*: "late night song"; *Inertia Magazine*: "looking for signs"; *Parting Gifts*: "the bad season"; *Sleet Magazine*: "bells & bones"; *Yew Journal*: "of humans & hawks"

The poems from *Some Words Suicidal* (Cervena Barva Press), copyright © 2014 by Stella Vinitchi Radulescu, are reprinted by permission of the author. The poems from *All Seeds & Blues* (WordTech Editions), copyright © 2011 by Stella Vinitchi Radulescu, are reprinted by permission of the author. The poems from *Insomnia in Flowers* (Plain View Press), copyright © 2008 by Stella Vinitchi Radulescu, are reprinted by permission of the author. The poems from *Diving with the Whales* (March Street Press), copyright © 2008 by Stella Vinitchi Radulescu, are reprinted by permission of the author. The poems from *Last Call* (March Street Press), copyright © 2005 by Stella Vinitchi Radulescu, are reprinted by permission of the author. The poems from *Self Portrait in Blue* (March Street Press), copyright © 2004 by Stella Vinitchi Radulescu, are reprinted by permission of the author. The poems from *From Heaven with Love* (Pudding House Publications), copyright © 2003 by Stella Vinitchi Radulescu, are reprinted by permission of the author. The poems from *My Dream Has Red Fingers* (CeShore/SterlingHouse Publisher), copyright © 2000 by Stella Vinitchi Radulescu, are reprinted by permission of the author. The poems from *Blood & White Apples* (Mellen Poetry Press), copyright © 1993 by Stella Vinitchi Radulescu, are reprinted by permission of the author. The poems from *Blooming Death* (The Golden Quill Press), copyright © 1989 by Stella Vinitchi Radulescu, are reprinted by permission of the author.

contents

new poems
(2014)

from
diving with the whales
(2008)

from
last call
(2005)

from
self portrait in blue
(2004)

new poems

(2014)

*To one who stood outside the door, one
evening:*
to him
I opened my word—

    —Paul Celan

word came

word came

over my chest,

a big cross

extending its power,

fleshless sound

over the visible

world—

my mother speaks so:

I can listen   can't stop

the flow

silence

pouring from her mouth

lessons in diving & thirst

inspiration is nothing compared to the long
road   : revelation   each mouth speaking
another language
give me more time   more space
the glamour
of the day:
I'll be there light as a feather   we
the only birds buried
in flight

.

who is the ghost whose steps are   a guitar
playing
remember the place the crowd the spring a body
looking for you o, the story
never unfolded
music still hurts I am so loud calling your name
it happened to be sunday—
sunday like an old song
dying

.

the slaughter house still exists   : on the hill
a hawk like a thought
of dull eternity—
slavery of light   I am meant
to survive
the shock of one tooth against another grinding
words
could you come closer
closer
to this spot

of bloody encounter

·

you said bring me a drop of water
in your palm
the thirst of the earth
the red umbrella on the beach
splashed
in images of sounds   a tiny
swallow just flew
over my head   I am happy
and don't know what happiness
means—
children as ever
nothing changes in the changing
of clouds
I brought you the sea
you wouldn't drink it but drowned

·

what took so long to open this window
and look outside
diving
the sea under your feet
houses torn down the past the king the rat such
feelings—
like a vulture like a child they flew out of sight
the well crafted things
of the world—
blackbirds are another story they stay late
and sing
softness from forgotten souls   have you

seen on the kitchen table the knife
and then the rain
washing away my wings & my hair

bells & bones

douleur[1]—

a knock at the door,

a finger cut off becomes

a simple word

say it,

say it again—

the world is watching your

bloody tongue

lifting the weight

of silence

.

brother again   the oak—

panic

through windowpanes of darkness

human configuration

of time   : arms, arms falling

---

1   *douleur* [French]: pain; grief; distress

& rising,

flowering   : speak

to this mouth   the long due summer,

the sky,

the language   ours

lost

in the grass

·

death pays off

familiar faces on the wall, cheap frames

& all—

cut out the rhyme

glory is greed, and nothing

sells for free

your hands are digging the grave:

here comes the farewell

the heroic horse

8

the timeless music of the soul,

bells & bones

late night song

after singing. after tears.

silk silk. soft colors.

silky worms. creeping.

shameless stars.

shimmering night.

water under water. the highest point of a prayer.

it seems. it dreams.

waving from where you should come. kissing.

missing.

the prayer. the water. the kiss.

so goes the wound.

my addiction to you.

heart heart heart

I went broke   nobody
helped my soul
to recover.

if I were You   your bold your blunt desire
your latest make-up   a foliage—

silver sleep
running in my veins
like holy water   : I remember
the town, the street,

something called *past*
better than the unbleached sun,

the broken sounds
heart
heart
heart:

sit down angel,   I am desperately alive.

looking for signs

Ce qui excuse Dieu, c'est qu'il n'existe pas.[2]
    —Stendhal

I should make music from your amnesia

God

should go into the woods looking
for signs

a shovel a tune a feather
in the dark

                    back to earth your skull & the wind
                    ravaging the trees

I keep singing keep walking on

I escaped saintliness

---

2   [French] "God's only excuse is that he doesn't exist."

self portrait in black & white

I am your closest friend when winter blows
and takes you away—

your body, full, exposed
to this language

of mine   a shadow follows
each word—

as before my beauty soars to love—

I hate when coming back some days
I have to tighten my hair, give up my eyes,
my lips,

the damaged face of time.

divine the body

divine the body took the stand
against divinity

the Book of Hours on the shelf
the dust of days & nights

I learned to shiver in the wind
and how to be a leaf
when fall

is falling
out of breath I also learned to fly

I can go far as far as death—

now winter you can come

untitled 1

eternity might fail
the test
of the forthcoming
night

: so deep inside
so close
to beauty   as tears
to the eye

untitled 2

how close is close
how green
is green when light
forgets
to shine   and birds
are stuck
in flight

or you
with deadly
hands
you push me into life

untitled 3

the truth belongs
to those
who never say
good-bye

or lie about
being
here   in love
with falling
gods

untitled 4

the agonizing sun
said no
when I was trying to hang up
my clothes

and my belongings   the rope
of days
and days to come all of the sudden
broke :

to be
for one more
night
instead of centuries
of dust

untitled 5

the rhyme is mean and tells ahead
the plot
before I even think
to lay it down

it litters all I have to say
or hide
on pages with no
end

while ending is the only way
to start this newly
settled
day

ennui

it's sunday,
past saturday,
past friday,
Rilke died,
my father up
in the sky,
the cold,
the question,
the who,
the why,
the human
blood, that
heavy load
and cold again,
and heaven
in full size.
the cross, the
nails take care.
take care of
your craving and
decorate
the room with
honey-
suckle
and angels.

story of us

if talking present childhood green

or fuchsia

the future of the race

it's quiet in the cemetery

thoughts skeletal

clean

washed by the moon

west of the western world the wharf—

he plays guitar

and we dance

drowned in our own sea

old manuscripts

weeds

your tongue as an omen

metaphysics of numbers

five days in a row

five is good   it demolishes

four

four seasons four directions

of the wind

the squared world

in one corner I found myself

sleeping—sleep—an echo

passing through

leaves

leaves of dark   *this*   you

and you

under my tongue   innumerable

dead

feline like rain

music from an old age   five fingers

touching the strings:

the earth returns to sea   the sea

to stars

of humans & hawks

Look! Look! he is climbing the last light
Who knows neither Time nor error...
    —Robert Penn Warren, "Evening Hawk"

there is a feeling a common feeling in the air
about our day
our life about almost everything that starts
burning our
eyes

moon
ice in the mirror   : if you are

here following the flight
the hawk's flight as we did
in our time

orphans   a father
not mine nor yours   : humanity haunts our town

the cell phone beeps twice

snow starts falling

what we feel   *not because*   emptiness
at the end of the line

22

the city of Dis

*. . . and I saw on every side a great plain
full of grief and torment.*
—Dante, *Inferno*, Canto X

1.

I like the sound the flowing from far away

longing for me.

someone cries inside—

my ears cling to the swamp   that heat

in each vowel.

Medusa's languid smile—lungs

deep

receivers of time   but who:

who are you expanding your memory

upon

my breath

no velvet shroud no lids on our days—

days open to us like new graves.

2.

the sun doesn't sleep
the fan doesn't fan
the guest speaker doesn't blink

we pass the Styx
we fight an angel
two
if you say *heaven* it takes some time
to absorb the dust
—plot of the day

they increase the heat
the rate of inflation
and sinking into

sand
and full of hope
and it doesn't matter

teaching death to fourth graders

I teach death to fourth graders; I start
with A—the *Apple*—the madness
in the Fall—
worms,
sweetness coming from inside
I want them to touch the crisp, the pouring
autumn light:

this is Adam, I say,
his blood,
his hunger & thirst—I am a two-legged
phenomenon
diving in the space we have—
the white whale
who lost her way to redemption

I teach the smell, the bad seed, the rotten
smell of words:
Sep-tem-ber   say it until you hear
the angel—
my child still to be born
sugary sap drips in his bones

I teach colors   long gone colors
& sounds:
hummingbirds, peonies, ashes, and rain—
strip and don't move, your mother
will come to you
with white baskets—apples—the crop
for years to come

I teach eyes, open eyes, closed eyes,
eyelashes, lips,
hands to grasp, and hands to let loose

a couple of things—
late night feeling of something we haven't done:
something
we haven't
lived

the human condition

after Berryman's Dream Songs

1.

so Henry went to sleep, you know Henry, while still

at the barber shop

clipping his nails with small nail clippers,

in the closet above

towels and french soap—are you hiding a knife

in your dream does the embryo have memory—

the clock just hit the floor

ten—bang—who is Henry would he go further

2.

he was a boy and then

he wasn't

a poet took him away drained his blood

his ideas   he was screaming God

make me invisible now as I am losing

my hair and everything else I could

for the rest of my life

stay put under my bed covered with clouds

and fresh leaves

as I was when I was dead

3.

I lost Berryman's book and now I have

to make up words

to imagine the setting on a page and how

the world works

how he chooses his friends his clothes

so many flights between life

and death

so many blanks

4.

there is charcoal in clouds

and bread on the table. something to say.

easy words.

little space on the moon. what happened

to Henry. did he say I love you?

back home the kitchen the stove.

yes.

the chair is black. with white wings you can.

you can sit on.

house of nowhere

my house grew small one day—

a mound

on yellow-brownish ground

as mentioned in the history of earth a tiny place

to shelter us

two windows at the right   the sun—

next came the winter

and I the keeper would have left

the spot   instead I decorated all the rooms

with red petunias sprigs

of blood

and wrote it down the night the stars

the crazy vowels

of the wind   —the house was rising

to the sky—

who doesn't know that I am here buried

in light

was god with me when I said *yes*

was god with me when I said *yes*

and *no* after

the flood

flowers switched to beasts and beasts

to clouds   *Les Fleurs du Mal* not yet

released

but I was happy I could speak the lost

unspoken

time

and write on paper the unwritten world

even the blind could see

a spark

two words colliding in the dark

asleep between words

1.

or gold and silver branches littering

the sky

we used to call them winter but when

the winter really

came

and bells of cold were calling us—

we fell asleep between

words

as big as mountains in the sun as small

and white

as flakes of dream we used to call them

snow

2.

and time that never stops—

it stopped

a full hole in your shoe   you—

go ahead and fill it up with roads

and rivers and

all along

the warm smell of your blood

I close my eyes

the moon has risen I close

my eyes

to keep inside

the last drop

of dark

sweet dark   you sleep?

the dog—the drum—the sin

rain didn't come

an army of dead trees

invaded

the town

elegy for my first day

Perdóname, Señor: qué poco he muerto! [3]
  —César Vallejo

it started with a move
from my head to my toe   : diaphanous
the thought
of it—

such urgency in what comes next,
no tenderness no mercy in these veins,
in winds in wars that shudder

the ship;
voices growing vague, beauty in a cage
a pig is worth the genius skull—

if you look through
the wall
the surgeon goes underground   days

won't heal
let's picnic on my grave   I inhabit
a witch

a fat idea of *what*   from Heidegger to

my finger, the red carpet, the glitter—I try
not to cry,
not to step back:

I am mending the death with a thread
of blood.

---

3   [Spanish] "Forgive me, Lord: how little I have died!"

a word for this and days to come

where are you going asked the man with
a hat and a scythe

uninterrupted roads went on in autumn
greed
and yellow light

some were asleep in the beauty of the sun,
some following us—the pattern
of the day

and days to come
next to the river passing through another one
bigger and bigger

that makes more sense   : a word for it—
the other one got lost
in dreams.

a drop of woman blood

and now a drop of woman

blood:

I swim down to the moon

the four horsemen greet me

with a smile

I follow   : nothing ends

with a pale vowel

the I

soaked in twilight in bitterness

in gold

the coffin—

the cathedral   some people drink

from my palms

some

forgot to wake up

resetting the clock

he took the knife
from my hand the rose

from my heart—
black rain

in a cup
I reset the clock

to a smaller
round   everyone

is not meant to be here
alive

a squirrel or a god

evening love

my love is the little star

drowned

in the swamp

song of a frog   a splash

of light

a tiny road to nowhere

let's call her

Ophelia

no

so what.

trees are speaking in tongues
my father rakes dead vowels   waiting
for the summer
to come,
we also
speak
a foreign language:
no to roses, *no* to bees
they are not
ours,
we are not here

the planet crashed and nobody survived

the heart

listen to it   : blood pumping out
the wreckage.

grace

So much depends. . .
  —William Carlos Williams

my presence in the room
stirs the birds:

they fly

slightly bent towards me
the horizon:

an eye or two I climb
the view:

two sparrows make love in the sun

the day is meek in secrecy

the day is meek in secrecy

is brewing blood

like wine

whose empty glass waits

for me

so far away—the distance

growing

by the pound

    —where are you easy cozy lark

such heaviness

in clouds

let's listen to Mozart

one   two   three

numbers evolve.   we are birds,

we are ugly,

we are old.   overused stones.

numbers here, numbers there.   who counts?

I am fed up with my ghost:

she kneels where I should kneel

and talk   : a mouth for every human being,

a sound for every leaf—

let's listen to Mozart and get lost in the air,

for I see you again

crossing the road.   you are coming my way—

saintliness and beyond

: the parallel mind

call me Ishmael

*Yes, these eyes are windows and this body of mine
is the house.*
    —Herman Melville

call me Ishmael

and looking far away and disobeying

time,

knowledge rises   blowing

winds:

at the bottom of the sea I should exist

and hold the vase,

salt thirst, mortal desire—

and floating so on upper floor   the monster

and the sea:

two eyes in one—the phantom dies

and dies

keeper of dreams

for my sister

the house at times stays still

across the street

not moving wings or lips

in northern

winds

my sister sleeps in me I let her

dream my dreams

she speaks in tongues   some words

I've never heard or seen

keep coming so

in flight

new birds

new eyes within my eyes

all dressed in black

& white

like day and

night

daydreams

Prospero: We are such stuff as dreams are made on.
—William Shakespeare

all colors in my hand

am I leaving the place am I seeking

forgiveness from no god or the clean world gets cleaner

tell me the story

download your pain

when it happened the dreaming   the long poem

: arteries & veins

                    •

bring water and then your thirst as if alone with a body

of yours

little time to live—

would dreaming bring relief to those not here legs & arms

in the field   I see crows

snakes hawks interfering in words— as if not seeing

                    •

48

what is the noise the engine   music   broken Corelli

cracks in the basement sucking

& stocking shifting us

to tears—

green tainted with sleep   wake up, monster, it's day time

bits of light and teasing suns   atoms colliding

on foreign land   unless the beginning

didn't yet start

                    .

light & shade & whispering names we came—whose turn—

ours

why not—everything blue on top rusty at the bottom

the wheel the clock

tell tell   time runs out of time

what a rush—

I could be the Eye could be

the owl

watching you all night

.

dreams are human beings are they—

do they fly do they have wings to carry the body over

the sea

home of sirens & long nights of sleep—

forgiven bodies invisible wings

the bad season

the bad season starts with a twisted tongue

west of the country I have lost:

losing

takes you to another word   sweet melody of the night

my ears

my ribbons of darkness   I could have been your name

hallucinating in a place like this

: a mouth

speeding into namelessness

howl

oh, life, panther in my rosy bed

floating on high

waves   star after star descend

the hill of time

with no lantern in my hand

I am hunting you down

I take you

back to these words I keep lining up

keep howling

rescuing

you

from the flood

the penal colony

after Dawn at Cayenne[4] *by René Magritte*

1.

to find the exit, I built a door

where life should end where life

should start   the island empty,

clear the day

all executions at dawn.

if you knew, God, how much I doubt you

you'd make an angel of me to drain

the wound,

the blood all over the place.   mice

roaming in your brain:

they get things right   stars don't fall

in vain

2.

the turnip was what Beckett said,

---

4   Cayenne Penal Colony (Bagne de Cayenne) in the French Guiana

the food for those who wait

and wait—

he took a bite and put it down.

his view differs from written sounds

further than that,

he said adieu.   strong light on stones,

the bed on waves,

minutes, like cockroaches, piling up

on the floor

in corners at the edge of spoken

time

they can't escape unless—

the chamber moves from here to there,

where phones are ringing,

where you can't see the end.

3.

five times five years of war: insomnia

grows from wall to wall.

hide your face under your bed, hide your

possessions

your soul.   is it you,

the girl I was,   you black feather

in the wind,

black snow?

it's going to be final:

final and cold.   we don't have time,

we don't have any time,

we don't have time at all.

lullabies of guns

in the open field   and your forever

eye.

4.

at six,

prefix.

dial the number—

seven, the shower, the cat

on the roof:

last scene of creation.

skip eight,

execution at nine,

short break,   button

your eyes,

all ends at ten,

le jour se lève[5]   : mother

to be,

mother to tell.

---

5   *le jour se lève* [French]: dawn is breaking

do you hear my silence,

it's me me me le sans-coeur.[6]

some words suicidal

(2014)

I, of whom I know nothing, I know my eyes are open, be-cause of the tears that pour from them unceasingly.

I invented love, music, the smell of flowering currant, to escape from me.

— Samuel Beckett, *The Unnamable*

these words are bees stars ants

these words are bees are stars are ants roaming
on the page

beyond understanding—

.

or the absurdity of footprints

.

I faked my face but it came back
in thousands of beautiful
deaths

the illiterate soul   sounds falling
like snow
on closed eyes

philosopher of chairs clouds eggs

I see a chair he said
the brain
philosopher of chairs clouds eggs

just at the time when flying
upside down
it was dissolving
in particles
of light

should I continue or just die—

or you can touch it
with your tongue he said in all
the languages

I know—
I tried to get it back in place in fact
in time

around my disappearing table

some words suicidal

. . . *l'arithmétique mène à la philologie, et la philologie
mène au crime. . .*[7]
—Eugène Ionesco

if you are still playing on the ground
still dreaming of a long
blue sentence
you may be using the word *sand* or talk
about your sister
your friends
little hands building the square face

of the moon
or want to jump
or say good-bye childhood too long
my hair grew wild
until it reached
the end
another danger *time*

and flying back don't dare to open
your mouth
you'll be swallowed up by hungry sounds
the rope too short
the sky too far
if you say *this* or *that* you might be burnt alive
your ashes

already here beware
of the word *now*

---

7   [French] "...arithmetic leads to philology, and philology leads to crime..."

what remains

she is my mother still alive
and well in my late winter
sleep

her talking mute   mute
as a dream

a silenced tongue
is worth the rhyme
smoke goes upstairs and

into the sky :
I deserted you one summer
afternoon

when comets like children
were playing around
but eyes and flesh :

your eyes your flesh on the page
I am reaching your hand   you have dropped
mine

ode to a swan or to imagination

swan of the last man
imagining *a man*—

like you
floating in dense air snow wings

snow mind   it's hard
not to think

not to love what really is
or isn't

the naked hand the body mirroring
its absence

the blue regresses to life—
days after

and days before
I woke up as a song

plainsong

if you are here
in front
of the door
you are the time
the story
to be told
your trembling
lips and
heaven
slipping through
your words
dead
or alive
the heart gives
back
the gift
of life
the shiver goes
to bones
and wanes in flesh
your sleep
or our sleepy
waters—
the wrong moon
rises
over the plains

Chicago and the rest of the world watching the moon

The moon is the mother of
pathos and pity.
    —Wallace Stevens

Chicago and the rest of the world watching

the moon

the whaling the sailing the glitter

thousands of years ago lost

in the thicket—

theme & conclusion as we talk

and vanish

in our own words   a poet thinks it's time

to shower & shave

time to sit down and write a moonlight sonnet

our heaven

our heaven

our dogs eat from

the same

evening pot where

the sky dumps

a full bag

of stars

I have this vision

of all the visions

at once:

sentimental

like the moon

I ride the hills

and delete

the return

lovers in winter

black waves are winter waves
the green came later
with a splash

of light

our eyes bigger & bigger   we were
lovers in winter growing
young

with the wind

we are humans in spring   pink
and blue bodies
streets turning to dreams—

stay tuned

colors may change   god was
off-white
now

poisonous red

nostalgia

What is returning?
Nearly nothing, but it could be a flake of snow.
—Paul Celan

if I am getting somewhere it would be
a place like this
that fits
in the moon   solid light

an apple
a skull wrapped up in jasmine fragrance—
once I was a fish
in your friendly eye

after all we are not the same nor
different
from our gods flowering yellow or blue

in the yard   *we are supposed*
to be the guests—

if I am getting nowhere it would be
a place that fits in your mind
a very long sentence

or simply
a word   if I called it wind
it would roar

behind the black fence

the music tickles the roof
in the garden beyond the black fence
they are trying to find
a way out

she climbs a tiny shadow
that circles the oak
he knocks at the invisible door
between purple
and red

there is a mist in the air like sweat
desolation comes in fine
steps
searching for the grass

they can't touch while shameless
gestures of life
are pouring down
with the rain

Paris in sepia

it's like a beat in my head

cold weather and soupe gratinée

once in a while a poet throws

himself into eternal

life

the Seine takes his body

intimacy

late afternoon coming again
they come and pass
late birds
from undisclosed

skies
you move your chair next
to mine
between us

a breeze of time

how do I look? —naked
framed hanging
on the wall
a glass of wine in one hand

bread in the other   : what has
to be grasped
what has to be said

I use the monster trick and pass the Styx

imitation of a man so he will never fail

he sits in the Museum of Rain

triangular made out of small gestures

sand

flesh & spirit a crack

in the stone   captive like god

in his own name   resembling

a ghost

the meaning itself—

/ my dog reads Dante and gnaws

the bones /

the king the analyst sexologist of time

stuck among umbrellas

and mice

a man of honor honoring

the dust—

74

I step aside

I go by days by numbers and silence his tongue

the origin of music

Things as they are
Are changed upon the blue guitar.
——Wallace Stevens

light comes from the rear window except sunday morning—

too far too cold

and the craving to write about things

things as they are

saliva as a sign

an image leaves the body

where are the clouds?

the baby sucks   milk spilled over the page

o night o music   small mounds

of earth

the nipples suck back:

 no punctuation

mammals with wings

if you dare

short encounter

made in the air
by the air the hour   / bring your

shovel to bury me in its shade /
narrow as it is the window

doesn't allow the view to shine
the wing

to fly   we need more roses
and then more words

to call them such

listen

the noise the bleating of the stars
who wants

to carry the world—

/ who cut us off from the answer /

Renaissance

flying is a matter of style

silence will strap you on earth

the Renaissance gardens won't fit
in your eyes

but remember

you are still a clod in my hands
I can mold you

again

.

the skylark took off—

the blue grew higher the world grew deeper

one can see the bottom of the day
migrating

mother, how I fear you now your huge eye
from which soon

winter will come

pastoral view

the trail gets loose in cold imagination

loose

losing

lost

the cock-a-doodle-do the egg the panoramic view—

but leaves were real little tombs and warm

the day under my feet

must have been

spring

I said tomorrow

you said yesterday

trees rising to the sky like candles   lips

that take the shape

of the moon

slow song

I imagine myself sitting on the porch writing this letter

to you

moonlight and all—

as if nothing had happened to us both on the same side

of the hour

the pen in my right hand   a slight inclination

of the planet

slides down the paper   : it came so close to your eyes almost

inside the frame

the language I was using never again the same

april fever

for Marie-Thé

let's sit down & chat   the last two chairs

of the season start moving

backwards   let's hold hands & go crazy

about each other's eyes

under our feet something final

something big echoes   desire

and loss

the midnight song

the roaming stars

let's be silent sitting there like two frozen angels

in the square   come   come you rose

that bled in my eyes before night

before the freeze

let the world go on let the spring come

nude in the snow

the flesh starts with a song
snow starts late night talking of white—

somewhere a wound

: the goddess with no arms and human scars
instead

the bleeding rose

the garden

.

the moon has dragged the body behind
your eyes

the nude not really nude

the difference is time

what you should see   the healing   white
melting

in your mouth   the flame
loosing power

in flashing sounds

malaise

the sister I don't have starts
drinking my blood

the man I don't love keeps
coming into my dream

strangely true these roses
of death

like truth itself

a poet dying seeks refuge and
sets the page on fire

tea time in heaven

we painted the room
in black

silverware on the table
black cups black

hands
ready to grasp

we painted some birds
on our plates

and then
we ate them

alive

it was yesterday

I was walking
neither on Earth nor in the sky
empty eyes fullness
in one hand
don't touch me said a voice touching
my lips

—as in a coma
pale & more pale the lady
with hollow face
enlightens us
again—heat was coming

from old snow
a melting tongue oh, Come on girl
don't leave me now or lose
your hair

the next day it was yesterday   the sin
the art of not being

barefoot I stepped on the grass already a dream

all seeds & blues

(2011)

the name

going round & round the day starts—

the blessing

where

when

whose steps   *letters in the sand*   isn't that

me

my   shadow walking   by the lake

      ·

let's remember

a day a season a street rushed
to the end

the mirror on the wall my face is small
and pale

one wing fell to the ground

the other was taken away   trying to call it

stillness like blood
in the air

I overspelled my name   things are like this

they just never seem to be

spring fugue

spring came
storming
the eye the hour
the magnolia
the sun

expandable
beauty
up to my tongue

the goldfinch
the snake
rise
to understanding
hushed
the voice of the past

the consulting room

how is your breathing asked
the doctor and held the stethoscope
close to my heart
I had in mind another thing
a chill an open door   I seldom
act as a rat

something buzzing over my head
was it enough
I appeared to be red on the screen
a muscle a short figure obsessed
with life sitting

there and nowhere else no breathing
likewise
I looked outside it was silent
and dark and I said
thank you doctor for telling me
that I am dead

valse triste[8]

stay away from my song   it has thorns

all along it says how I was born and then

reborn   *mental hygiene for humans*

as they go on   in winter and how a

whirling tune   thousands of voices

in a big ball   let's go as far as silence

takes us   kneeling on emptiness

I am not   coming back

the time of saying this :   days and nights

     wild & mortal

---

8   *valse triste* [French]: sad waltz

the longest summer

that violent summer

with no end

ended in words:

time wasn't for living

I am overwhelmed by this lightness
my fluttering past

he is my mother my father eventually

my unborn child

an open field   crows
hungry for sweet souvenirs

Poe on demand

It is rewarding to live in no time   defiance
good for the climate

I am on my knees

bleaching the lingerie

sanctifying the floor

paysage[9]

take me to the beach where the air is music
the place for our bodies
to be at large
nights

and days then more
a minute
a second the full range
of things

keep me as I am
dozing on warm sand mouth open

you can call me

eternal

       •

the lobster keeps up with his hunger
digging the sea

Dalí in the air

me too
I found the word for *sadness* and the word for *joy*
happy
in their flesh

more or less

let me start again

---

9   *paysage* [French]: landscape

mimophilia

wearing your body
moonlighting the hills sunbathing the streets
cutting roots with your eyes
trimming the hours

the silky scarf around my neck let me have
your morning dreams
your divinity
I'll pin it in my hair

unbutton my dress I am hungry
I am blue I am not the meaning   your hands
the cold

I have such an appetite for snow

one wing at a time one death

orangerie.com

here we go again with the blue
swamped with seaweeds and beauty
the holy splash
long floating
violins

I hear the music I see the sky moving
but touching no
the octopus retracts
am I walking too close

or maybe too far from when I first saw the flight
Nymphéas on display
I have to stop I have to tie my shoe on the way
to school

the pond
viciously white oh,
how I love the black swan the only one not there

elegy for the rain

the train leaves the big eye   the blinking
night in your hair
the cigarette
dying

the rain implores
: nobody comes back   didn't you learn
the rules of ascension
leap

upon landing
on a soft cloth of dreams
the sun is down
his jazzy
bones

make a wish, human, on your dust

playing chess

1.

I don't know the rules I go erratic   to see the sun
I drive east where I left my shoes

under the bed
my raincoat on the chair

a woman keeps telling the story about a piece of land
taken away

spring came
the heart went the other way

the queen
has been put to rest the golden casket is filled with
sand

2.

I play the queen and you love me and cover my body
with decadent art   the painting
in plain view

those who are blind shiver   those who are deaf
speak

their hunger

indian summer chases the seasons   don't think
we are done with the dogwood
blossoms

all seeds & blues

one sound and then another trying to put together
a day—

the red apple

the roundness

one eye and then another help the light
to break in

: you and me we are holding the vase
with no arms

do not disturb the sleep

all seeds & blues she waits in the shadow her teeth

as luminous as hunger one bite
then another

: somewhere
the snow covers the night

stone bed stone air

I was neither there
nor here
a storm of years left me
on shore
sleep like milk spilled
in the sick
house
the woman haunted
by her own
heart
stone bed stone air islands
of eyes flowing
backwards
the pillow slips away
her head
a scar that grows
from the unwanted
flesh

just now goldsandaled Dawn

> —Sappho

just now goldsandaled Dawn:

the deer came closer to my hand
looking for
flowers

a mother maybe

the sun far west in tears

but this is not really the case not now

not here
an image in a cage of sounds

the grazing
of stars

death by exposure to dreams

chamber music

sunset or dawn
the story starts with a window
cut on low winter sky

interior of an unfinished fruit
the womb
a day between us in love with our shadows

a touch like water you still here?

lips flowering black spots
on the wall
the violin dies in a remote spring

the orange or the blue dress I would wear

half world

until the last word is said

landing on holy silence

if you think it will take
months and years
to start moving and breathing

: *alive*
in the country of blue

music pouring from the ground
a silhouette
ashore in fluid words
the sleepy horse of time...

     •

more life coming from the street the child
the scream the squirrel
the language
we invent

exotic clothes hang from the trees stop
walking in my eyes

resurrection
needs no more light for you to land
on holy silence

ballets russes

have you ever seen a ghost
the trembling of the house / space moving ahead

shape of a skull

beauty in its final stage

: trophy down
it's the end of the war

small feet on the ground tulips
and daffodils
the trot

trottiner trottinant[10]
the pavement of death

                  ·

Nijinski in red
let's bury him in his own flesh
face up
solid all across

from right to left *glissando*

wet   wet floor

we were children in a remote time
mothers like angels
flying around

---

10   *trottiner* [French]: to patter, to scurry (present progressive: *trottinant*)

Peace on Earth nothing to talk about:

people in our town—
they are still building bridges of blood

retreat

in one sound

enough space to build

your summer

house

briefing your life

late evening

under

the stars

enough time

to catch the last

flight—

Tristia said the poet

and then

he died

september sun

when we planted the oak
it was september
spring in Brazil
winter
under our feet
nineteen days after the making
of the planet
no time that I know
took roots
in her grave sleeping
face down
not to see not to be touched
a sigh came out of
the ground
shoveling worms
dirt
the tapering light
winds split us
this blood on our hands
branches
and leaves
in numerous parts
this september sun

in static waters

last move
what to expect the dome of hours floats
away

there is a feeling about

[. . . . .]

next

the broken line   the snake

wakes up to see

the bruise

        •

springtime again and we are due
for love

in static waters there is a sign that slowly moves
to knowledge   oppressive as the sky

could be
it promises relief   what we can grasp

a word or two
on ever

dying
lips

insomnia in flowers

(2008)

for my parents, in memoriam

scream

I went too far, too far in the woods. the tree
was there, the body hanging
from a branch.

it was yesterday, I was looking for God.

free from gravity, his legs in the wind
right, left...
a creepy balance between shadows and light.

too far on earth, too far into the night... I touched
the corpse, it went away in flames
and dust.

he is still there in the declining moon some words would fit
his skull

and I was scared, the scream
took my whole body with it, I thought I was flying...

but no, there I found myself stuck on the ground
from scream to scream building
an altar of silence.

the voice I don't have

1.

the voice I don't have is the voice I want,
yours,
broken in pieces, spread out on the floor, hot shower
along the spine

your voice, star, trembling at the edge

2.

and yours,
tall man with the afternoon light in your hair,
separating humans from gods,
one finger from the other...

voice that roars when the music stops

your voice,
little dead mother, they nailed your coffin,
lashed the night,

they nailed and nailed until something went wrong,
sounds returned to their place
and merged into one word

spelling loud

there is a crisp sound in the air
                                         earth moving

a day going on

tea sugar on the table
violet sky in somebody's eyes
                                    a room
in the room
my flesh in yours   thank you mother

thanks for taking me back   for the fresh leaves
the language I speak once a year when the sun

digs you out   cherry trees in blossom again
rehearsing a new death

spelling loud your silence
                                  a short yes
flowers for teeth

teeth for flowers

temptation

1.

horses in a dream the rain doesn't stop   saints with sacred
books
reading to the stars

horses get involved   the story of life   why not run away
why not come back

nothing starts here but horses

2.

in a dream with horses

the rain doesn't stop   saints with no books reading your mind
you
in a dream

history of words   the word for rain the word for horse something
seen
heard

something to be cast

as blue as racing time

news from my backyard

we are together—

the feeling comes from the leaves
yellow and red
all the same in our eyes

from our shadows beating their wings
against the sun

a moving figure of life

and echoes of *I love you* carried by the wind—

being alive

here

at this hour

.

who created the world—

I promise you to make a small change

one word I'll whisper
in your ear

even if the wind will take it away and you'll never
hear it

this is how silence sounds in my yard

•

I lie down and look at the sky

I see my thoughts rising   they fly around
then stop

make in the dark little holes for the stars

the way crickets are burying silence

•

first it was a sound

then a shape moved in the grass

it scared me

it took me along

old bones carried away by clouds

stars are like children

it was so hot I couldn't open my eyes

a stair   the armchair   universal care for poets

he said

in time of war

it should be prose

hard to listen or follow the road

not a road

but five fingers diminishing to one

that's all

I heard from his perspective

under the stars—

stars are like children

playing with us

sky was a joke in our late conversation

a man lighting his blue cigars

with Stevens' tie

french lesson in the garden

peel the onion   layer after layer after layer
of white

words won't hurt as the first snow
comes again from Villon's hell

roses with long necks swans floating at dawn

democracy needs more poppies
more red

pause   café crème   between two leaves
of grass

yellow comes by surprise like Christ
with a cut off ear

playing Ophelia

I write for you, I drag you into this line,
in the space I have I rush you, I cover you
with letters, connect you

to the title.
I write because I can't touch you,
I was at the gate and you didn't come. I wasn't there

and you came with flowers,
I called your name, nobody answered. night comes
with a loud scream vomiting stars.

I hate the way you are not here
wearing your black shirt, the way you whisper my name
with no sound.

let me exit, my hair scares me, the stage is full of rats,
my thoughts are old, older than me,
give me back the fog, the loneliness, the body I forgot

in your cheap dream.

sweet amnesia

I am on my way to the door

open it

it's open he said and closed his eyes morning came

and the sun

blinds me   people run out of food

out of time

they don't remember don't talk don't rush

they are missing their turn

to something better cheaper more beautiful—

I forgot the name of all the birds

how are they going to fly?

who killed first and lasted for ever?

sunday at the beach learning foreign languages

1.

I put on my sunglasses to look like
when I was twelve.

romanian time. they were digging a corpse.
a drowned man.

from that brutal silence.

he was covered with weeds, shells, swollen, black.
children nearby were playing ball.

the horizon

a dark blue line.

storm on everyone's face.

2.

I bought a beer at the end of the deck.
I sent postcards to my friends. red umbrellas, women
with big hats, ecstasy in the air.

the horizon came closer.

the corpse deflated.

time filled with sand.

3.

I am still learning the language of death.

Mozart's Requiem

they have lived a stone life, a star life, a rat life,
tears wiped out by the Siberian wind, packages wrapped
in despair,
moved from prison to prison, from age to age.

we used to bury our people, carve a cross, play Mozart's
Requiem,
they started a new era of solitude
and loss,
their corpses our trees, our roads,

tons of blood evaporating in the air we breathe,
corpses lost in the tide of all times, high tide
on our empty beach, the grave

we don't deserve, the thoughts we never thought.
most of you don't even know why and for whom you are crying,
don't see their faces, don't hear their trumpets

when they happen to pass by your door.

1955

to scream once it takes seconds;
to scream twice it takes hours;
to scream for ever obliterates time.

Nothing wears black watch and plaid shirt
for special occasions

like when the father was taken away,
melted snow dripped from the gutters

spring was about to come...

      •

and we still have these words
bare bones and barbed wire in our souls,
lost imagination

outdated chromosomes drying up
on the plate

dark pleasure. lips in a cage start singing the anthem—

who are you at the beginning
of the century
to be asking questions about happiness?

learning the map of the world

1.

we were naked
on naked unlit streets
young and old not knowing our age

yet knowing the fear that was overgrown
with the roses

2.

we were in school learning the map of the world
just at the right scale
bodies surrounded with walls of deep water
and fiery dogs

but sadness felt so good in the warm rain

and we were happy to break our lives into small pieces
and give them away
to unhappy strangers
forgotten

coffins nailed on sunny streets with no sound

rough winter, cold meals

it's snowing, freezing, cold meals, shorter days,
people get disoriented, scream, hide,
go to war, die.

someone on top, on the roof, the basement
full of water, the flood.

Amen, I hear a voice from above.

my husband and I we came from a foreign country,
our pictures too dark, our clothes still unpacked.

or maybe we never arrived.

there are times when voices are filled with rage.

there are times when the rain is red.

there are times when you are a woman and you think
somewhere in the room there should be a place
where you could hide

a place where you'll never die

life syndrome

what I say is dead wrong
who I am is a mistake

are you here? remember, we are born the same day
same hour same mother
same father   who gives directions who chooses the day

blink
I blink
smile
I smile

people think I don't even exist how can I prove you are
not me how can I
kill you
with your hand
this is what confuses me, the lack of rules, the sky too big,
the kind of heart rushing to catch my breath

everything in one direction, one lousy dream...

numbers and leaves to rake

raking the leaves
dear you, I found myself wearing your coat and your shoes

better times on Morgue Street

We existed within ourselves alone.
    — Edgar Allan Poe

remembering the cold   off white   crisp
in our summer heat
they blink in the dark they are not yet muted

nor asleep

there are dreams all over the wall spiders
and exotic palms climb the hour

dressed in a long milky robe I move toward you
on this tune of smoke

                    •

he forgot his hat

she forgot the lipstick pale as a star

undressed in the mirror but

on the other side there is plenty of time

nights and days to be returned

footprints of life

                    •

crows know better the cloning
I could be inside   a thought already freed

floors gradually removed

new species
and the heart follows broad patterns
of disappearance

     ·

who talks in trees in waves in tongues

a noise like long awaited wings

memory eats from my hands

claws the heart   human

emptiness

who knows the price

     ·

open area for you to invent the speech

of love

from almost nothing that exists   pleasure
and pain   not even a casket dropped for us

to be swept or hailed

in small waves

1.

fall is here, the music is gone,
count the dead birds, look for someone you love.

I have no memories of writing letters to you,
the postcard all wrinkled still in my purse.

thick and muddy the night covers the floor.

2.

over and over rolling the sun onto the beach, seagulls like us
cross the land in despair.

one boat is leaving, another one at full speed
approaches the shore.

we move in small waves.

on turtles & death

nothing told me that I will soon die

my hands are in place

my legs

the book in front of me breezy

waves brewing time

from the heart a bric-a-brac of old
toys   nothing to be stored

on the other side

.

in my dream I was a turtle with blue eyes

rolling my shell in exotic waters

death like a twister

I dragged myself out of the sea

my black sisters the pearls conspire

against me

distort the limbs

new ritual in hiding   deepest layers

invention of speech

•

the high tide leaves more verbs on the beach

I draw them all over my feet   they whisper

I am on my knees

an exercise in learning   hand written letters

for tall priests

Descartes would like to see me naked

chinese leaves are good

for depression

cold the brain half-aware

•

I am your landscape of death my lover you

your picture in the room

the skull of life well crafted hung

on four golden nails

sunday no mail

frozen news   the night expands

extinct volcano

magma

I want to turn on the light the gesture

doesn't reach the hand

                  •

the ocean flaps in my face   salt and memories

a house burns on both sides
of Earth

a tiny envelope floats on waves
heading undisturbed

to nowhere

132

what remains (2)

1.

and I move again from here to there,
one step ahead of you, exhaling like the ocean
on the hot summer sand.

for moving keeps me in place,
clean and beautiful. keeps me from being who I am.

evening sits in front of me like a porcelain vase.
all birds sleep on one branch

faces like ours fill up the empty space.

2.

to be there is what takes me here.
I see a squirrel crossing the street, I remember myself
in a day like this, the smell of spring,
a fresh gooseberry

crushed in my mouth.
fierce words are seizing our children, our trees. what remains
doesn't speak.

I am stuck in the middle of a thought...
happiness, what is your name?

winter talk

love is a ghost   let it inside   welcome

the winter   dress it in white

don't talk   listen

·

the first drop of rain is yours

finish the sentence

days like hawks hover

souls unborn

adjust their wings

·

the mind wears black not knowing why

one little hour sits in my hand

I see you coming with the storm of years

curtains flow crimson

windows go drunk   I see you tall   I see you running

sleeveless as if ready to lift me up

intermission

and all the roads took us to the Black Sea
always before dawn   the sand
still wet
seagulls sleeping in the air

where is everyone you once asked
and looked around

one by one stars were leaving the world
we were leaving our bodies

each moment postponed to eternity

it was long before time

insomnia in flowers

I was walking on a narrow wonderful
small road

stepping on rocks looking for answers

I went to the edge of one thing

I found nothing

my house floats backwards on the river

a child in the garden opens
black wings

·

who should be here

to whom do I speak

who lost his tooth in the green of the ocean—

I dip my hands in the night

nobody starts crying

·

don't talk

insomnia in flowers

a blue silhouette that could fit in my dream

what I can't bear any longer

the smell of the moon

the music of untitled poems

diving with
the whales

(2008)

We have lingered in the chambers of the sea
By sea-girls wreathed with seaweed red and brown
Till human voices wake us, and we drown.

—T.S. Eliot

if I remember

amazing grace on ugly days as if
I have been sold for time

on the way to the market the birds:

they go back to their nests   the thunder
hits the bottom

yours the knife

      •

if I remember it is for forgiveness

you speeding and I behind picking up little sounds

the sinful trumpet

the gods and you speaking the same language

      •

lavender evening

ghosts approaching the shore

I follow their footpath   I almost

hit a star

diving with the whales

the pilot whale like the pilot light keeps our sea from
retracting

wide open the shell of time

I keep talking talking cut my way through the waves

the whale joins me   white for the teeth

crimson for remembrance

stars browsing through the lost pages

Le Déjeuner sur l'herbe

after Edouard Manet

we sit in the sun with white plates in our hands

far away a tune fades in the air

our lives go by

.

at sundown my mother bakes the bread : flour, salt, water
with her fingers she works the dough, makes a little hole,
sets the yeast in the middle.

later on milk from the moon. her grave shines by the river—

o, mother

night up to the end,
country of all forgiveness

the gate was open

the gate was open but my hands were cut

late afternoon

we were having a party

some were asleep some not

some throwing bombs from the roof

the sleepers watching from their sleep

I was looking for something

forgot the language

a funny noise under the oak, mother?

despair and joy

one says that cut off from the world the body

still keeps breathing

zone

and then she cried cries would cry
will cry   verb after verb
for the baby yesterday
in her arms

for not having being able to reach and hold him again
for not being able to hold
the woman she was

in the garden

or the garden itself

wrinkle after wrinkle the earth cracked
her face blew up
and the night
threw his heavy coat over the house—
brightness

always fades away
vowels turn into broken consonants
this is
what
I
remember

unless
something was real   like the flesh
in its absence
rush

rush to see me

the statue is already in your eyes

the blue screen

waiting for you to write me again
those words
pushed into numbness

the space between us uncanny
and unaware

to figure out a letter or to open the womb
there is always someone
who takes care of the unknown
waters the grave

thoughts are timeless weightless

what about wounds

new look the corpse

the crazy man is not crazy enough he thinks he is alive.
his neighbors buried him when it was the case. the sun came
down.

children were watching. I was watching. you maybe were
watching too.

oh, honey,
I said, *death fits you well...*

between squalls of northern wind he smiles and moves his
feet.

not dead enough, walks on the street, takes the bus,
still has to pay the rent.

life gets more expensive every day.

new look the corpse between leaves and twigs.

what goes around ends in a ditch.

complicity

in front of the window the big tree fell down
cars stop at no sign
little by little

the notebook swallows my shadow I see the crack
disappearance of one finger
then two

I play the ghost I feed you   bread and wine
sand and snow:

up to your name I have to climb
this Everest of light

time for an angel

everything one thing

wounds   leaves   clouds

the light changing   a sound

far away

longs for my lips

.

they come they come all wrapped
in secrecy

the dead army

I remember a loud sentence   vaults

falling apart

and my face in the middle and who cares
if I speak

speak twice the face I should leave to the wind

driving home, forsythia bushes in blossom

I think I know who I am unless you forgot me,
a draft of air took me too seriously
and swept my body away

I remember
flying over your head in a tiny shell, smell of seaweed,
a couple of clouds...

•

back in womb.
a tear in a yellow crust.

I am driving home, forsythia bushes in blossom,
why do I cry why do I cry

imagine the world destroying the world—

light switched to dark.
I remember being nowhere,

unless you saw me flying in your yard.

ritardando

first it was the hair like a black pumpkin
on top of the head then the man the trumpet

drops of rain

a wheel-chair speeding in the afternoon light

and the noise in my chest

·

beachseagullshoneysuckle and all…

a cavity

the engine hum & hum the wind doesn't stop

a thought ahead

I almost lost balance two boys bicycling
they let me pass it's like a bridge

a bridge in the air and I have to rush   colors
slip out of my eyes

·

the neighborhood has changed, my dear, the boys
have put away their bikes

the sky beneath you

the sea left us—

as if I was trying to come back   as if
I had slept a thousand years

starting point

1.

at the beginning of the light
the clock was set to this very moment
a road was cut

life didn't happen for centuries
then my parents came and gave me flesh

here I am   a heart made out of frozen seconds
a second itself freezing in front of your eyes

this is what makes this moment alive
my body to grow
to seek understanding

2.

and what if I fail and what if I don't
the day is not what you see the apple is not
what you want

desire keeps dripping around

this is how it is, the big lie which makes us feel
good
about our selves

forgive me for talking in no voice
for not bleeding peacefully like the sun

3.

the answer is in our hands

but we don't understand   a long time ago

we named things at random
now we are paying for it

we don't see a soul like we see the moon rising
we don't understand simple facts
where are we going
why do the seagulls cry   I have these words

sometimes I feel like touching their flesh
the roundness

and then I let them fall
one by one into your mouth, Mr. Nothing

make me an offer
I will buy your big and burning eyes

4.

now is the moment for the tide to rise for you to be here
to ask and to cry
to be young to be old to check the weather
to bury your friend

now is the moment to make your bed
go to sleep

doucement doucement[11]
falling into a long dream

---

11   *doucement* [French]: softly; gently

·

mirror of clouds
no whisper
no hidden meaning under the shrine
nothing about snow
about us gripping the dark

we have learned the music

a second lit in our palms

from where we stand

from where we stand   let's say the valley
saliva rises
we should talk   sunset and butterflies
fire on top of the pines
hills sinking
in sound
up to the throat the wolf the illusion hysterical
clouds
slightly left looking from inside somebody
a woman
waves to us and we could almost be there
lay on the grass word after word
listen to the echo

deepen the time

last call

(2005)

for my daughter

my father gave me his name

my father gave me his name
I am stuck with it
if I move it really hurts   a body
still afloat

if I open my mouth I feel like spinning blood—
will the birds come back
will you start breathing again

if today's light falls on the page
I might go on with the pain
you left
a little box where love and hate

made their nest   sometimes the rain
washes off a letter or two
I hear a voice

neither yours nor mine coming
from an empty grave

history

a chair and a window
the rain
you

take your turn
take into account the room the light
your face like sliding in a ditch

the edge of something scattered moves to the edge
words are ecstatic
the day rustles

the phone rings and goes into history
so does the picture of the two boys
on the beach

dusk falls on earth and all you have to say
fits into the eagle's eye
ready for another rotation

hotel tristesse[12]

a hat for my left foot   shoes for the brain
click on me
say hello with your snappy eyes what

do I know about you
occasionally I take you into my house

hour of mine, lay down
lay down

hungry for love I light a candle in my mouth
letters burn
burn and then fall

ashes along our little dirty world

lend me your tongue
I buried mine a long time ago
there was no place for such a flame

angels soaked in sweat and blood
a heart dropped at night
in this mud

---

12   *tristesse* [French]: sadness

moonlight sonata

sweet comes from ashes   bones
in the sweetness of sleep,
diffusion of dreams. adjectives
picking up from the ground a color, a sound.

summer on the kitchen floor makes dirty waves, the boy
next door still practicing the moonlight sonata.
he gets stuck there, always there, the long arpeggio where
the wind reaches the linden trees.

we are on our way to salvation, we definitely have
blue hair, blue eyes as many as birds—
meet the monster licking the hour from the plate.
he wants to smash it, the immensity.

I have the power to say no, I have a body that fits tragedy,
when I am green I sink in the Atlantic,
yellow makes me look like a snake.
no heaven, no metaphor.

first I was a voice, then a flame, then the idea of flame,
the ghost. if by any chance I am god,
I'll take the night for granted
and sleep on the couch.

purple

I have a purple face you see
the damage of the purple wind I was playing with one summer
in a remote town

it was a shortage of hot water and colors
your ID, said the man—he looked at me
and put a purple stamp on my face

it went inside like a tattoo ran down the veins
puddles of silence small streams
of time

it's somehow the color of being alone

         •

to be chaotic to be exotic to be erotic   small needs
from big sounds
the urgency of a purple word

I believe in you as a mirror
I believe in long nights, short days—

cover me with your breath, your purple disbelief
I am not from here and I feel the pain

my heart unfolds its daily song
as if I were happy

last call

I call home. the phone rings.
far away a man stands still at the door.

I am calling from the station, mother!

the voice makes loops, circles the streets, plunges inside:
empty house, echoes of small animals running on the floor.

the last train was leaving.

now. they are pouring wine and boiling wheat.

they sing. make strange noises.

the phone rings. I rush to answer, someone pushes me away.
a candle. the old carpet.

green and red birds are filling the sky. I am at the station,

hello?

corpses last, they don't talk.

black curtains

black curtains. the curtains are black.

I have never seen the light. may I call it a chair,
a red chair by the sea, the immaculate cloud—

tristesse du soir sur le balcon:[13]

the balcony with a small view,
earth growing old and older

a window opens.
people I know from the other life
are pumping beauty on the grass

and sleep in golden veins of time.

what happened to my body? I was wearing
my daily gown half-flame

half-shadow.

    it's not my time,
white snake,
take it from me and put it back in the trees.

---

13   *tristesse du soir sur le balcon* [French]: "sadness of evening on the balcony"

afterlife

when I woke up it was already afterlife.

new worlds were picking up like winds.

how it could be?

you came last night,

we were well tied, the sky was on.

I am not here or there or simply I am not

or maybe only words are tearing us apart...

self portrait in blue

(2004)

before dawn

I take the stand in front of you,
my body, old tree,
grown from an undisclosed time—
sky pours down like jazz,

a festival of stars between two ribs
talking to each other the sweet language
of ashes. fall comes to my mind;
wandering in my mother's eyes,

green first, then yellow, then red,
keeping up with the music,
the branches, the wood burning inside.
inside of inside, me too, like a vulture.

my mother opens her eyes,
the music stops, the planet bleeds,
my image staggers in disarray.
the pain comes later with the body,

a word I can't spell.

from one word to another

1.

from one word to another
I am alive
I flow on my breath
I am my grave

a flower comes to life
a ring encompasses
the remains
of the spring

my body
a full body of sounds
stands up
on the hill

2.

from one word to another
it's winter
close the window
sleepy rooms along
the road

the sky still gray
full of uneasy sounds—
sit next to me
in the deep velvet hour
fit the night
in my eyes

3.

I found the water
on my way to the well—
it was at night
little moons were hanging
on long stalks

no one else was alive

Modigliani's red

1.

present into past. a small sky vanishes
like an old spot on the wall.

I stand in front of the sun, walk between lines,
I touch the air with my lips: bruises, bruises,
Modigliani's red over my face.

2.

past into present. space into time.
my parents came a long way only to be
the desert I can't hold in my hands.

am I searching for something to find or to lose?
wildly sad, diffused, beautiful,
a tactile absence, a virtual blue screen
withdrawn from human eyes on which only once...

at the station

1.

the railroad was white with heavy snow.
my father stood still in a wooden frame,
russian, buttoned tunic, my mother wore a black dress
for the ball.

was it yesterday or today? was it during the flood
or during the war?
was I too little to know I was alive?

then I could fly like a kite, lie down on the kitchen floor,
the smell of stars in my hair, I could separate seasons
by looking into my mother's eyes

2.

the railroad ended in a small station, men and women
took their bags, crossed the tracks...

time stops here, announced the loud-speaker,
my parents were smiling in an awkward way,
I touched them, I waved and waved,
the picture blurred...

time for the heart to take over whatever remains

flood

you are not alone and you are alone under the lonely sky
with your glory in your back-pack wrapped with your shirts
and your shoes,
with the world shrinking in your throat.

you are not alone and you are alone with your few words
frozen in your heart, the light frozen in your eyes,
an invisible hand moves the queen
from white to black
and the day breaks on your shoulders.

you are alone and you are not alone in your death,
stars are watching you. we will take your back-pack
home along with your glory.

evening comes too early, windows shattered by strange
winds.

we are waiting, still waiting for you here, around the table,
we can't sleep or cook dinner tonight, your blood
has flooded the sink.

another day

coffee and dusty thoughts the shower runs red everything
runs red except my blood which little by little
turns white

I keep toasting I keep pouring water into purple cups
I keep forgetting the past look at my fingers
they don't fit my hands anymore

a man brought me flowers he died before I opened the door
breakfast for one   one full second   one inch of time
the dove owns the space between my eyes

how far from heaven do you think we are?

yes and yes, no and no   perfect setting for love
I am trying to compose a sensual smile
the mirror takes over
it's a mask

touch me   hours will die hours will swarm
another day like this will come

not enough words

not enough words
empty lines hanging like severed hands.

the flamingo the fish and the finch
are the same
not enough space for the sun to rise.

streets longer than dreams
days and nights eaten by ants.

one more thought stumbles
in the dark.

pray for the stone pray for the ash
we are like gods
grazing in empty yards.

self portrait in blue

easy to be here with you
in the room easy

to be a room full of blue easy
to be blue

in the afternoon and not to be
a saucer a spoon

an eternal cloud heading north
heading south or

a flying thing in a robe that stinks—

I am serious I can eat wear a hat
pick up an apple empty the trash easy

to be in a dream and to dream
to like the sun when it comes out

to like these people they almost dance
when they are not sleeping

or buying guns then a new rhyme
and the dream goes away easy

not to sit on a bed of hay not
to walk around with three hands

and three legs a dime in your mouth
easy not to have this blue face of mine

sunset

where should I go to see another sunset,
no vessels leaving the shore, no funerals.

it happened at once on a small scale of change,
disappearance into disappearance,
elements sleeping like strangers one next to the other.

the swan crosses the hour.

someone at the end of the road should have been
as human as the night which descends
without expectation,

without a knife.

what you told me in front of the house,
who you were then with your warm wet hands
of desire
all went back into waves, stone, shell.

pieces of history standing inside demolition.

the next sunset is what we are looking for,
we, who were born in this elation of time,
nothing else could have happened to us.

redemption

I have built a house on the hill
with little stairs   little hours
where I am kneeling to worship my death

when evening comes I clean the air
and dust the sun in the yard   night eats light
light eats light

a reversible word is on my tongue:
what I am trying to say is already said,
already dust

there is no way for you to find out—
sounds die in their own flesh   as long
as this phrase goes on

we can't split our tongues, my lonely,
hungry father
give me again your seed

seed for a finishing body,
my heart like an old city lost in time
rewords memories   you can see

leaves on the ground you can hear waves
and strange winds,
eventually get used to the sound

of your own heart

from heaven with love

(2003)

for Alexander and Nicholas

after killing a blackbird

one day I will be free again to tell you
the story of my life,
to invent the day, the hour, the place it started.
I will be free to say, she is my mother, he is my father.

my first day on earth...
I remember everything that happened to me,
how god, with one of my hands, mixed life and death
in a bucket, how scared I was and I asked
what if we can't separate them again?

free to love you, to touch you with the other hand,
the one I kept for life,
I remember, I was free to be free,
to die free

before someone killed a blackbird
and the night fell upon us and covered the earth
with a long shroud of sadness.

late journey

if you can't find the end of the road, the place
where the tree you planted as a child
turned into a cross

and you don't have a choice between two
or several days to carry on your craving
for a word big enough to cover
the place you are looking for, if you don't find

the end of the hall which takes you to oblivion
where things are hungry for your eyes
and you start dropping them one by one,
if you don't hear the noise, the beat,

the falling apples in the fall—
it is because you didn't start the journey
and the green keeps on retracting,
too early for redemption, too late for ecstasy;

each word says something and something else,
who said I could be an angel if I learned
how to fly, some ideas
go far beyond what they mean.

in slow motion

1.

stars in slow motion descend the airy stairs.
children talk loud. loud blue.
blue-jay finally comes across my eyes.

small thoughts lost in the grass.

2.

whose kingdom is that?

stars in slow motion fly back where they belong.
black holes.

I have nothing in my arms.

somewhere the clock has struck ten

if it's too soon to tell you this
it's because it is sunday
and the moon is deeply wounded and the night is roaring
and everything in the air is coming to an end

someone said god
someone pushed the door

someone was green someone blocked the window with a
scream
someone arrived someone went to a far away end of the deck
and threw a coin in the ocean

someone stayed in the middle and cried

somewhere the clock has struck ten—

our planet is one inch behind the time,
a bird couldn't remember his song, a flower
forgot the spring

and light, a huge piece of glass crashed in my throat
like something I would like to say
and no word would come out of my mouth

in the middle of the river

in the middle of the river there is a river
flowing backwards,
from death to life and then to the first day
where the flight started, where we first met
as intergalactic birds, naked, wounded, bleeding,
shining...

who are you stranger whose joy rolls on my tongue,
like a bead of fire
as I look at you, you enter history through my eyes
or maybe myself multiplied by hundreds
will be our history—

ours, ours, slaves of human power,
of gravity, of hunger,
parts always wanting the whole, whole always
scattered in parts—
and I might end up in one fluttering wing,
this sound, this bubble bubbling around, ah, it's all waste
and you are asking, what did you say?

I am trying to raise my voice up to your tongue,
to fill up the gap between one heart and another,
I am already a part of my corpse,
a tiny letter in the book you have just closed.

the golden fleece

the day is sticky
the music sublime
the plants are dying
the summer stinks

doors are pink or blue
the golden fleece is lost
you can't open the window
unless you are god

I am grateful to you
little snake
for bringing this light
to an end

japanese gardens

1.

the eyes were little stones
the little stones were stars
there was no sky
no earth
we were all blind
with flashy hands
exotic flowers
whistling loud

red was like lighting a candle, pushing the boat
all the way to the sea
no bird could alter
the sip
the music of the shifting
sand

2.

to be at the edge where
tears
give birth to the eye
to be the wall
between two meanings
two flowers
two stones
it's a place called
loneliness—

3.

black & white bridges
hanging from the past. a sound crosses
the night
like a flying dragon

walking on sounds, on the smell
of burning comets
and skulls
takes us to the entrance

my dream has red fingers

(2000)

simple touch

isn't that me   my image
over there
coming out from the mirror,
growing
pushing with sharp rays
the hour the air?

isn't my breath the spider
weaving my presence thread
by thread
a painful burning wing
which rises from the glass
and fastens
on my shoulders
made of ice?

angel or snake

the metaphysics of love
starts here
with a tiny movement
a shiver between two blades
of grass
nothing

but a sound
angel or snake
like an old music
coming out
from the ground
why

should I cry in the twilight
and rush into the dark
tears
turn to a new light
a new question
a small

word on my lips
            healing
                time

"O soul, you who go on to be happy..."

—Dante, *Purgatory,* Canto V

eating earth along with
the stars is now the privilege
of the dead
but a word in my mouth
like a swelling mound still
measures the distance to the
lost sun

•

Angel, for you I am here
in the middle of the shining wound
waiting for my body to bleed
to blossom
to give you new invisible roots

•

I imagine you lost in your own emptiness
and the wound in my chest
grows from your never recovered
presence

suddenly alive

day night day
night riding
the invisible
horse:
suddenly
alive

peace comes like snow

peace comes like snow
from the heaviest
clouds
traveling west traveling
north
foreseeing the storm

new memory   a new song
approaches the soul

are we the end or the beginning—

what is white and light
will touch again
our hands

when my words

when my words
were in prison I used
to see them every week at least
two or three times
bribe the guards or simply
break the wall
with my teeth:

extremely cold and rough were
the vowels   children of hunger
and loss—
someone said something about
a party going on
in the world

I can't remember how long
the winter lasted
mouth and throat
already full of snow
today
I am still shoveling
the road
waiting for those words
to be set free

sometimes I find blood
on my handkerchief
and I think
this is how we are awakened
from a long
long sleep

every day's chill

every day's chill
and the love I was longing for
brought me to this big
skeletal city
neither heaven nor hell—
however angels are taking their turns
in my dreams
and devils take my silence
as granted

I have learned to forget
and to fail
I have learned to walk on empty
unfriendly streets
to talk
to say hello to strangers

I have met names and names
floating without bodies along
the lake
stones
    unfinished lists like those
in Saint Luke's cemetery

I have experienced the spring
without your violet-bluish
eyes and the smell of forsythia
but most of all
I have learned how to carry
under my tongue
a small sound   a bead
with the sour strong taste
of the yeast

my mother used to knead
into our daily bread

my truth is behind those doors

my truth is behind those doors
where we used to live
and die
intoxicated by our own movements
and thoughts—
fear and smoke
no one could ever
take a deep breath
or a walk by the sea
the Black Sea   where
one day I discovered a woman
buried in waves   with long
green legs
dark starry eyes and
my own face

dear mother

still snowing purple winter eyes
my blood keeps wiring the time
violins of rage on each window
each grave   none of my souls
is willing to rise

still snowing winter purple eyes
my words keep digging the silence
at the bottom no wrinkles no tears
perfect world drawn into its own
blood

but one day one day I won my life
from you from this dark: stop crying
in my flesh stop dying in my
hands dear, dear mother

elegy

to arrive at the new house
to pass the hill
of your absence   to hear
the crumbling
of things
the same light which wrinkles
the clock

to arrive at the same new
place
where children are dancing
for the last time
where leaves are turning
into graves

only in agony the world
revolves

I should say snow

the green turned to black
the black to white
I should say snow
but the word is like
blood
doesn't show unless there is
a wound

a wound in the middle of the silence
I should say in the middle of the heart
but the heart just turned
into a sound
a vicious helpless music between
to be and to die

blood & white apples

(1993)

The dance along the artery
The circulation of the lymph
Are figured in the drift of stars
Ascend to summer in the tree

—T.S. Eliot

about gravity, about stars

from now to never   from
you to the grass   from
your hunger to a tiny heart   all
air all earth   go
go to the edge and your body
will follow

·

I am in danger by raising
this voice
moving slowly through flames
I am consuming
my own flesh to light
this illusion
again

·

slavery never ends: it is
our strength
to go from cage to cage
to believe
we are meant to fly
to be birds

·

a flying woman
could tell the truth
about gravity
about stars
good manners and dirty
eyes

about being here
on earth
about the urgency of love

I, the flight

learning the sounds from the beginning
to death
lining wall to wall the silence

raising a voice from one to the limbo
from terror to mercy
getting closer and closer to my arms
to my legs

blowing up gravity the heaviness
of my flesh I, the flight
I, the evidence of the sky

now that we are seeds again

word by word I go to the end
branch by branch towards the holy
tree where the wind will come
to tell me the truth about
the whole garden

tear by tear I believe   I believe
in the abstraction of the light
while we are walking on dark
sleeping on dark   dark our pillows
dark our memories

piece by piece I discover your face
your hidden gestures—snakes
of hope
human retreat—
sound by sound I forgive
now that we are seeds again moving
faster & faster towards
the next spring—

I forgive your whiteness your
presence
balancing the world on the tip
of your tongue

facing this door

I am the only one facing
this door
the only one in the middle
of the expanding eye staring
at this door—
everything is behind it:
men and women in love warming
the earth
a bloody spring
a new flood
ecstatic waters carrying debris
of dead animals   twigs
words

I am the only one here
in the middle of nowhere
facing this door
I scratch the wood the holy wood
with my fingers
I miss your arms your flesh
the deluge
of your gestures
I am the only one on this side:
everybody in the house
died
long   long before I came
here
as a song

in dreary afternoons

in the beginning was the rain echoing
smoking
longing pains   then
came another day across the floor
one final word
choked in my throat

for each vowel of desire
a dynasty of angels will desert
my lips
in dreary afternoons
when light
pushes my eyes adrift...

plants for eternity

walking on empty streets like
in a broken mirror
the sunset splits my head in two
one purple eye   the other falls
beneath
the night

now I can walk like in a dream
on both sides
of time

·

peace is a state of mind as
the plain is a state of the universe
as we are plants for eternity never
dying for ever
since ever is a state of the soul
and now a state of my tongue

I rose from silence
and I can speak

the present moves

the present moves within
my hands
my fingers move within the page
new images arise
I share we share the sun
with the blind
what is ephemeral is meant
to survive
lightness belongs to seeds
which carry
our lives

blooming death

(1989)

dream

the earth is dreaming people
and moans
snow dogs are barking in our hearts
as if at the moon

go your way blue sorrow
blue pain
these hours are hunchbacked
by so many prayers

the earth is dreaming golden
big fruits
one bird two birds of hope
under the lost sun

give me your hand give me your
voice I have to pass
this smoky dusty word

pansies of loneliness
in the field

fall is eating like a bull
from our ashy souls

Genesis

a long
bright
thread
binding
us
to the
end

stone my tongue

words—
no one can move

no one can go farther
can die

stone my tongue   block
of time

underneath
your absence shivers

like a creek

love

you and me
ray close to
ray

the earth
is loosing
its nights

we are loosing
our names
which
one
is
us?

end

time is going away
and takes
our strength
we bite together
the very same
air

I dream my body
as a huge
void
into which someone
is throwing
me

I smile: one more wound
I cry: one more Christ

spring

IN
MY
CHEST
SOMEONE
IS
DIGG
ING
A
CREEK

snare

it's an angel, says the poet.
it's a dog, says the scholar.
it's my gloomy finger
looking for light
says god
while the day comes
at the crossroad of words
: the wind
the void
taking away our imponderable
lives

yes

yes, I exist
so far

my unfinished birth
is blinking
like
a star

endless

go and go
you'll find somewhere
the end of your eyes,
somewhere in the middle
of a tangerine day
you'll see the night like
an animal
coming against you

this is the end of my heart, you'll
say and it will be like the small
green town
in the mountains,
like all your hate
and your love,
like wringing the stars,
the voices you always
liked

and bigger and bigger
twin suns your eyes will hardly
find you
somewhere
in the middle of a tangerine
day
and you'll die again and
again

silence

I am the silence
don't trample me down
under your step
a word
like a snake
might suddenly
slither out

ars poetica

with my voice
I scrape
the window
of nothingness
like a small
child

new
pure light
is coming
inside

about the author

STELLA VINITCHI RADULESCU was born in Romania and left the country permanently in 1983, at the height of the communist regime. She holds a Ph.D. in French Language & Literature and has taught French at Loyola University and Northwestern University. Writing poetry in three languages, she has published numerous books in the United States, France, and Romania. Radulescu's French books have received several awards, including the Grand Prix de Poésie Henri-Noël Villard and the Prix Amélie Murat.